Psychopathogen

First published 2020 by The Hedgehog Poetry Press

Published in the UK by
The Hedgehog Poetry Press
5, Coppack House
Churchill Avenue
Clevedon
BS21 6QW

www.hedgehogpress.co.uk

ISBN: 978-1-913499-07-5

Psychopathogen

by

Nigel Kent

*For the millions
who have suffered from the Covid-19 pandemic
and for those who have worked selflessly to ease that suffering,
often in impossible circumstances.*

Contents

A TRAGEDY OF REVENGE

She cast us as assassins to despatch
the dearest of our family and friends.
Her mastery of murder's arts means
we need no knives, no guns, no pillows
to press upon our victims' mouths:
we kill with kisses and with handshakes,
spread death with baited breath
to entertain our mistress, Mother Earth,
who, watching her plot play out,
leans forward in her front row seat,
savouring the buttery-sweetness of revenge.

PSYCHOPATHOGEN

I'm a globetrotter,
skipping over
borders unannounced,

travelling incognito
though you'll know
I have arrived

when my hand
hooks into yours,
and won't give up

its grip;
when my breath corrodes
your throat;

when my weight
falls upon your chest
as your lungs flood.

President or pauper
you're all the same to me
just numbers in a sum.

You'd like to wash
your hands of me,
but you'll need to catch me first

and I'll ensure you do,
then slip away unseen
from the siren scream

to keep the total
climbing, the records
crashing, the headlines

coming and be
for eternity
the measurement of time.

GUARDIAN

When duty calls, he snoozes
on the chair outside the gate he guards,
his wings buckled beneath him,
halo slipped, covering his mouth and nose
like some makeshift surgical mask
whilst his belly, fattened with flattery
and swelling with excesses
of entitlement, obstructs the epidemic
of undesirables squeezing past him,
wheezing with the strain.

FEVER

When the sun calls
on her school-free mate,
to make the most
of his early release
by mucking about
in the locked down street
this wall climber,
this graduate of boredom,
sick from a surfeit
of internet sensations
and Netflix serials,
languishes in bed
with a fever so severe
he dreams of examinations,
of test results,
of crisp uniforms,
of patient professionals,
of the elixir of lessons.

HYPEROPIA

She told her husband she saw it coming,
had stocked up with toilet rolls and pasta packs
when supermarket shelves were stacked
though she believed it would be spread by birds, not bats;
'Being farsighted is a blessing,' she'd boasted.
*'The distant is so clear and the close
in soft-focus with all sharp edges blunted,'*
but Lockdown magnified as well as any lens
the grit chafing their relationship,
the many years of choking dust,
the cracks that made their days together sag,
and she resolved when things went back
to normal, she'd get her eyesight fixed.

"EMPLOYERS SHOULD TAKE EVERY POSSIBLE STEP TO FACILITATE EMPLOYEES WORKING FROM HOME," *GOVERNMENT GUIDANCE ON SOCIAL DISTANCING*

You are through to the office of mum and dad.
Unfortunately all our direct lines are busy right now.
Current wait time is approximately 60 minutes.
For an automated response to your query:
press 1 for menu and meal times;
press 2 for help with home lessons;
press 3 for entertainment restrictions;
press 4 for advice about difficulties with siblings;
press 5 if you have a fever and a cough.
For all other enquiries press 6, leave your name
and number and we'll ring back when available.
Thank you for calling the office of mum and dad
where parenting is our priority.
For the latest family news and events,
including arrangements for grandad's funeral,
check our Facebook page.

AESTIVATION

Just as nature was stirring,
waking from its winter coma,
they locked her down:

a housebound hibernation
with nothing to do but doze
before the still life of the street.

Her days defined by meals
and visits from the girls,
that rouse her for an hour or so

for lip-read conversations
before goodbye-hands sandwich
the window and reluctantly retreat;

hugs and kisses banned,
left at home like grounded
children who can't be trusted,

Too soon minutes start to melt again,
dripping into hours and collecting
in a stagnant pool of days,

when living is the smudge
of a handprint on the glass,
obscuring the bright sunshine.

A NEW KIND OF NORMAL

She scoured the papers and the 'net
for hours until she found it.

Not the direct replacement
she had been searching for;

her current model, unusable now,
no longer available.

A revised design on offer instead:
'*Ideal for life after Lockdown,*' it said.

Too soon for a user's review;
no choice but to take a chance.

It said it was Government approved,
fingers crossed it would be improved.

Yet when it finally arrived
she couldn't get along with it;

it was bargain basement basic,
not the super deluxe she was used to.

She'd liked to have sent it back,
but it was, '*Non-returnable*'.

ACKNOWLEDGEMENTS

My thanks to the following:

Kerry, Holly and Annie for their unflagging encouragement and patience.

The members of the **Open University Poetry Society** for their positive response to some of these poems when they were first shared at one of our Zoom get-togethers.

Mark Davidson, Editor of Hedgehog Press, for believing in these poems and giving them a platform.